The Country Bride Quilt

The
Country Bride
Quilt

Craig N. Heisey
and
Rachel T. Pellman

also "The Country Tulip Path Quilt"
and "The Country Basket Quilt"

Good Books®
Intercourse, Pennsylvania 17534

Acknowledgments

Design by Craig N. Heisey
Cover and color photography by Jonathan Charles
Author photo by Merle Good

The Country Bride Quilt
© 1988 by Good Books, Intercourse, PA 17534
International Standard Book Number:
0-934672-72-5
Library of Congress Catalog Card Number:
88-82139

Library of Congress Cataloging-in-Publication Data
Heisey, Craig N., 1957—
    The country bride quilt.

    1. Quilting—Patterns. I. Pellman, Rachel T.
(Rachel Thomas) II. Title.
TT835.H43 1988   746.9'7041   88-82139
ISBN 0-934672-72-5 (pbk.)

Table
of
Contents

The Country Bride Quilt

The Country Bride quilt was created in the spring of 1983. *Bride's Magazine* was decorating an old row house in downtown Lancaster, Pennsylvania, to be featured as a "first home" for a bride and groom. For the story the house was remodeled and completely furnished with accessories. Since Lancaster County is widely known for fine quality quilts, *Bride's Magazine* felt it would be appropriate to show a quilt on the bed. They wanted a special quilt—something original. It needed to be delicate yet sophisticated to fit the brass and white bed. It needed to be romantic and sentimental but able to hold its own as a strong graphic design.

They contacted the staff at The Old Country Store in Intercourse, Pennsylvania (10 miles east of Lancaster), about whether we would be willing to design such a quilt. It was a challenge we accepted with eagerness.

We immediately thought of hearts, flowers and love birds. These shapes suggested an applique rather than a pieced design. We sketched, revised and drew more sketches till the final pattern evolved.

Each appliqued patch contains a pair of love birds reminiscent of the traditional Pennsylvania Dutch distelfink. The birds rest above a heart which widens like a fan at its base. The hearts and birds are entwined in simple curved leaves brightened with delicate tulips. The applique patches are separated by patches of equal size decorated with plentiful quilting and an appliqued tulip in each corner.

Bride's Magazine fell in love with our design. The original quilt was done in shades of rose, lavender and green to coordinate with the walls, carpeting and upholstery of the bedroom. Photographs of the original quilt in its setting appeared in the June/July 1983 issue of *Bride's Magazine*. The original quilt now hangs in The Old Country Store, Main Street, Intercourse, where it continues to delight local quilters and visitors.

The Country Bride pattern is adaptable to small projects as well. A single appliqued patch can be made into a beautiful pillow. The patch is done following the instructions given for appliqueing. The pillow top may be quilted or left unquilted. To make the back of the pillow, cut a square the same size as the front in either matching or complementary fabric. With right sides together, stitch around the edges of the pillow leaving a five-inch opening along one side for stuffing. Turn pillow right side out. Stuff pillow. Handstitch opening.

A Country Bride wallhanging can be made using a single applied patch. Add borders to make the wallhanging the desired size. Quilt and bind, using instructions given for a full-sized quilt.

The Country Bride Quilt has been enjoyed by quilters and quilt lovers nationwide. Along with this *appliqued* design, The Old Country Store staff has designed and included in this volume, two original *pieced* quilt patterns. The Country Tulip Path Quilt and The Country Basket Quilt are here for your enjoyment!

The Country Tulip Path Quilt consists of sprightly geometric tulips, neatly ordered and separated by paths of sashing. The tulips may be arranged to form concentric rectangles (as in the color photo on page 72), or they may be set in horizontal or vertical rows. The tulip theme carries over to the border quilting designs where the geometric lines soften to curves.

Baskets full of flowers alternating with plain patches of elegant quilting combine to form The Country Basket Quilt (see page 70). Light and dark fabrics in the basket create the illusion of being woven. A sawtooth border surrounds the patches which lie on the surface of the bed. Geometric patches are offset by fine circular feather quilting designs with the floral motif repeated in the quilt's center.

How to Begin

Read the following instructions about either Applique Quilts or Pieced Quilts, depending upon which variety you intend to make. Be sure to read the entire appropriate section before beginning work on your quilt.

All fabrics should be washed before cutting. This will pre-shrink and also test them for colorfastness. If the fabric is not colorfast after one washing, either repeat the washings until the water remains clear or replace the cloth with another fabric. If fabrics are wrinkled after washing and drying they should be ironed before use.

Fabrics suitable for quilting are generally lightweight, tightly woven cotton and cotton/polyester blends. They should not unravel easily and should not hold excessive wrinkles when squeezed and released. Because of the hours of time required to make a quilt, it is worth investing in high quality fabrics.

Fabric requirements given here are for standard 45" wide fabric. If wider or more narrow fabrics are used, calculate the variations needed.

All seams are sewn using ¼" seam allowances. Measurements given include seam allowances *except* for applique pieces (See "How to Applique" section).

Applique Quilts

Preparing Background Fabric for Appliqueing

When purchasing fabric to be used for background and borders, it is best to buy the total amount needed from one bolt of fabric. This will assure that all the patches and borders will be the same shade. Dye lots can vary significantly from bolt to bolt of fabric and those differences are emphasized when placed next to each other in a quilt top.

Cutting diagrams are shown to make the most efficient use of fabric. Each piece should be labeled when cut. Mark right and wrong sides of fabric as well. Then lay border sections aside until the applique work is completed.

To indicate the placement of applique pieces on the background piece, trace the applique design lightly on the right side of the background fabric. Even though the applique pieces will be laid over these markings and stitched in place, it is important to mark these lines as lightly as possible. Center the applique designs on the background sections. The placement of the applique on the pillow throw is an exception to that rule. That applique should be centered from side to side but should be placed nearer the top of the quilt so that there is extra fullness for tucking the quilt under the pillows. The space from the top of the pillow throw section to the highest point of the bird's tailfeathers should measure 10 inches.

Making Templates

Make templates from pattern pieces printed in this book, using material that will not wear along the edges from repeated tracing. Cardboard is suitable for pieces being traced only a few times. Plastic lids or the sides of plastic cartons work well for templates that will be repeatedly used. Quilt supply shops and art supply stores carry plastic sheets that work well for template-making.

Precision begins with marking. First, test the template you have made against the original printed pattern for accuracy. The applique templates are given in their actual size, without seam allowances. Trace them that way. They should then be traced on the right side of the fabric, but spaced far enough apart so that they can be cut approximately ¼" *outside* the marked line. The traced line is the fold line indicating the exact shape of the applique piece. Since these lines will be on the right side of the fabric and will be on the folded edge, markings should be as light as possible.

Appliqueing

Begin by appliqueing the cut-out fabric pieces, one at a time, over

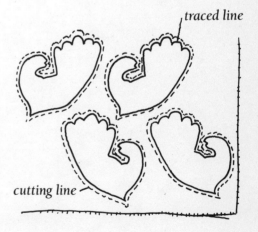

Applique templates should be traced on the right side of the fabric but spaced far enough apart so they can be cut approximately ¼" outside the marked line.

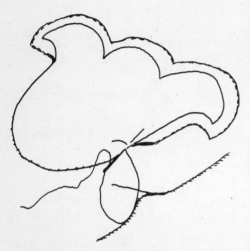

The applique stitch is a tiny, tight stitch that goes through the background fabric and emerges to catch only a few threads of the appliqued piece along the fold line.

the placement lines drawn onto the background fabric pieces. Be alert to the sequence in which the pieces are applied, so that sections which overlie each other are done in proper order. For example, in the fan section of the heart, begin by first appliqueing the bottom piece so the sections above it can be appliqued on top. In cases where a portion of an applique piece is covered by another, the section being covered does not need to be stitched, since it will be held in place by the stitches of the section that overlies it.

Appliqueing is not difficult, but it does require patience and precision. The best applique work has perfectly smooth curves and sharply defined points. To achieve this, stitches must be very small and tight. First, pin the piece being appliqued to the outline on the background piece. Using thread that matches the piece being applied, stitch the piece to the background section, folding the seam allowance under to the traced line on the applique piece. Fold under only a tiny section at a time.

The applique stitch is a running stitch going through the background fabric and emerging to catch only a few threads of the appliqued piece along the folded line. The needle should re-enter the background piece for the next stitch at almost the same place it emerged, creating a stitch so small that it is almost invisible along the edge of the appliqued piece. Stitches on the underside of the background fabric should be about ⅛″ long.

To form sharp points, fold in one side and stitch almost to the end of the point. Fold in the opposite side to form the point and push the excess seam allowance under with the point of the needle. Stitch tightly.

To form smooth curves, clip along the curves to the fold line. Fold under while stitching, using the needle to push under the seam allowances.

After appliqueing is completed on patches, embroidery work will be required for the stems, birds' eyes and beaks. Use matching thread for stems and contrasting colors for eyes and beaks.

Assembling the Appliqued Quilt Top

When all applique work is completed, the patches are ready to be assembled. See diagram on page 18.

To assemble a king-sized quilt, inside sections are added between Step 1 and Step 2. The lower corners of the inner section are mitered. To form the mitered corner, the ends of the borders must be cut at angles to each other. Measure in from each end the exact number of inches as the border width, on the right side of each border section. Using a straight edge, draw a diagonal line from that point to the outer corner. Cut along the angled line.

With right sides together, stitch the borders to the quilt, leaving a ¼" seam allowance open at each mitered end. The open ¼" seam allowance will be used as the seam allowance on the mitered corner. Stitch across the open ends of the corners from the inside corner to the outer edge. Backstitch at the ends to secure the seams. Proceed to step 2 in "Assembling the Quilt Top."

Pieced Quilts

Making Templates

The accuracy of a template will have a lot to do with whether or not a quilt fits together. Templates should be carefully traced onto a material that will withstand repeated outlining without wearing down at the edges. Cardboard is not appropriate for a template that must be used repeatedly. More durable materials are plastic lids from throw-away containers, the sides of a plastic milk or bleach jug, old linoleum scraps or plastic sheets found in quilt or art supply shops. Tin may also be used, but beware of its sharp edges. Sandpaper may be glued to the back of the template to keep it from slipping as you mark the fabrics.

Before you cut all the quilt's patches, cut enough for just one block by using the new template. Then assemble the patch to check for accuracy. If changes are required (perhaps the corners don't meet), adjust the template and try again. Always test the template by assembling one block before cutting fabric for an entire quilt top.

Marking Patches with Seam Allowances

This method requires that the template be made with a ¼" seam allowance on all sides. When traced onto the fabric, the marked line is the cutting line. The seam line is ¼" inside the marked line. The advantage of this method is that if you work with a very sharp scissors, you can trace the outline on the top layer of fabric, then cut through several layers of fabric at the same time. The disadvantage is that when you begin stitching the patches together, you will need to accurately guess the exact location of the ¼" seam allowances so that the corners of the patches meet precisely.

Marking Patches without Seam Allowances

This method requires that the template be made the actual size of the finished patch. The line that is traced onto the fabric is the stitching line. The cutting line must be imagined ¼" outside this line. The advantage here is that you have a tracing line to stitch along, almost guaranteeing accuracy in piecing. The disadvantage is

Mitering Corners

Step 1

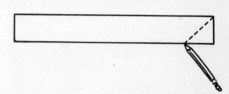

Measure in from each end the exact number of inches as the border width. Draw a diagonal line from that point to the outer corner. Cut along angled line.

Step 2

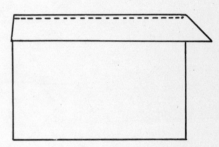

Stitch borders to quilt, leaving a ¼" seam allowance open at each mitered end.

Step 3

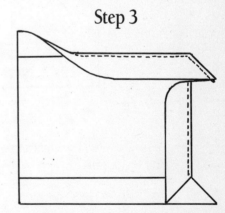

Stitch across the open ends of the corners from the inside corner to the outer edge.

that each patch must be marked and cut individually. With this method you cannot stack and cut multiple layers of fabrics. Each quilter must choose which of these methods works best for her/him. The important thing is to maintain accuracy by whatever way is most comfortable.

It is extremely important to be precise in marking and cutting. A very minute mistake in either step will be multiplied many times over when you try to assemble the quilt. Ultimately, you want to have a smooth flat quilt top. To achieve that, the individual pieces must fit precisely together.

Marking Fabrics

There are many ways to mark fabrics. You may use a regular lead pencil to trace the template. However, on some fabrics, especially dark ones, the markings are very difficult to see.

There are several pencils designed especially for quilters. Some of these make markings that are soluble in cold water, allowing for easy removal of markings. Some pencils make markings that disappear after a certain period of time. That works well if the pieces marked are used before the time elapses. Whatever you choose, be sure to follow the manufacturer's instructions for its use.

Piecing

You may piece a quilt in either of two ways: by hand or by machine. Hand-piecing is a more time-consuming and laborious process and most quilters today choose to piece by machine. However, when very small pieces are used and when several points need to meet, hand-piecing is the most precise and exact method. This way also allows the quilter to work on the project anywhere rather than being tied to a sewing machine. If hand-piecing is done, the longer straight seams on the borders and the sashing between blocks can still be stitched on the sewing machine to save time.

The hand-piecing technique is very simple. Pin the patches with their right sides together and with their stitching lines perfectly matched. Using a fine sharp needle, stitch with short running stitches through both layers of fabric. Stitches must be straight, even and tight to achieve an accurate and strong seam. Check stitches periodically to be sure they are not causing puckering. Put an occasional backstitch in with the running stitches to tighten the seam without creating puckers. At the end of the patch, backstitch and knot the thread before clipping. Open the patches and check the seam for precision.

When piecing, always begin by assembling the smaller patches and build them on to the larger pieces to form the quilt block.

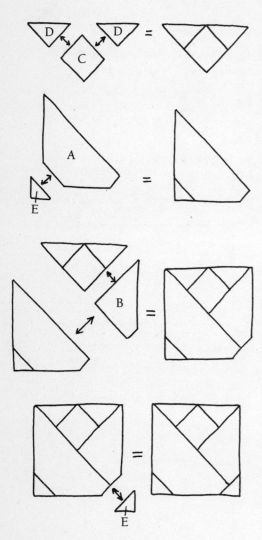

Combine patches to form straight sewing lines whenever possible.

Combine patches to form straight sewing lines whenever you can. You will want to avoid having to set in squares and triangles, if at all possible, since stitching around corners requires utmost care to prevent bunching and puckering. When setting in is required, it is important to stitch the patches that need to be set against each other only to the ends of their stitching lines, without stitching through their seam allowances. The seam allowances must be kept free to fit against the seam allowance on the piece being added.

There are two ways to set in a corner. Starting at the outer edge of one patch, stitch its full length (stopping at the seam allowance), pivot and proceed along the other edge. The other method is to begin stitching along the edge at the center or inner corner. Stitch from the inner corner to one outside edge and then go back to the corner and stitch the remaining edge. Practice both methods and use the one most easily completed for you.

Machine-piecing is obviously a lot faster. The procedure is basically the same as hand-piecing but the stitching is done by machine. Pin patches together accurately and watch carefully that they do not slip when going through the machine. In machine stitching there are no knots so it is important to backstitch whenever beginning or ending a seam.

Seam allowances can cause a problem when joining units of patches to each other, especially in two situations: one, if quilting needs to be done through the seam allowances making small stitches virtually impossible; and two, if a seam allowance of a dark fabric is visible underneath a lighter fabric. It is generally a good idea to lay all seam allowances in the same direction. However, if this creates either of the above problems, make an exception and lay the seam allowance the opposite way.

Quilting on Applique and Pieced Quilts

Marking Quilting Designs

Quilting designs are marked on the surface of the quilt top. A lead pencil provides a thin line and, if used with very little pressure, creates markings that are easily seen for quilting, yet do not distract when the quilt is completed. There are numerous marking pencils on the market, as well as chalk markers. Test whatever you choose on a scrap piece of fabric to be sure it performs as promised. Remember, quilting lines are not covered by quilting stitches, so the lines should be light or removable.

Patterns for quilting designs are included in this book. Since most spread over several pages, they will need to be assembled

Quilting lines are marked on the surface of the quilt top. Markings should be as light as possible so they are easily seen for quilting, yet do not distract when the quilting is completed.

before they can be used.

Fabrics that are light in color can be easily marked by laying the quilting design under the fabric, then simply tracing the design lightly onto the right side of the fabric. If the fabric is too dark or opaque to see through, a template must be made to lay on top of the fabric and traced through. This can be done by cutting thin slashes at regular intervals on the quilting design. Insert a pencil or marker point into the slashes and mark the lines lightly. Transfer marking paper can also be used, but care must be taken that the markings can be easily removed after quilting is completed.

Quilting

A quilt consists of three layers—the back or underside of the quilt, the batting and the top, which is the appliqued or patchwork layer. Quilting stitches follow a decorative pattern, piercing through all three layers of the quilt "sandwich" and holding it together.

Many quilters prefer to stretch their quilts into large quilting frames.
These are built so that the finished area of the quilt can be rolled up as work on it progresses. This type of frame allows space for several quilters to work on the same quilt and is used at quilting bees. Smaller hoops can also be used to quilt small sections at a time. If you use one of these smaller frames, it is important that the three layers of the quilt be stretched and thoroughly basted to keep the layers together without puckering.

The quilting stitch is a simple running stitch. Quilting needles are called "betweens" and are shorter than "sharps," which are regular hand sewing needles. The higher the number, the smaller the needle. Many quilters prefer a size 8 or 9 needle.

Quilting is done with a single strand of quilting thread. The thread is knotted and the needle is inserted through the top layer about one inch away from the point where quilting will begin emerging on a marked quilting line. The knot is then gently tugged through the fabric so it is hidden between the layers. The needle then re-enters the quilt top, going through all layers of the quilt.

The quilter's one hand remains under the quilt to feel when the needle has successfully penetrated all layers and to help guide the needle back up to the surface. The upper hand receives the needle and repeats the process. A series of as many as five stitches can be "stacked" on the needle before pulling the thread through. When working curves, fewer stitches can be stacked. Quilting stitches should be pulled taut but not so tight as to pucker the fabric. When the entire length of thread has been used, the stitching should be reinforced with a tiny backstitch. The needle is then reinserted in

A quilt is a sandwich of three layers— the quilt back, batting and the quilt top— all held together by the quilting stitches.

the top layer, pushed through for a long stitch, and then pulled out and clipped.

The goal in quilting is to have straight, even stitches that are of equal length on both the top and bottom of the quilt. This is best achieved with hours of practice.

Binding

The final stage in completing a quilt is the binding, which finishes the quilt's raw edge. When binding the edges of a scalloped quilt, it is best to cut the binding strips on the bias. This allows more flex and stretch around curves. To cut on the bias, cut the fabric at a 45° angle to the straight of grain. When binding a straight-edged quilt, it is not necessary to cut the fabric on the bias.

A double thickness of binding on the edge of the quilt gives it additional strength and durability. To create a double binding, cut the binding strips 4–4½" wide. Sew strips together to form a continuous length of binding. For a scalloped-edge quilt, this length will need to equal the two lengths plus the bottom edge of the quilt. The upper edge is straight. For a straight-edge binding, there will be four separate lengths—one for each side, top and bottom. The two lengths on the side will need to have an additional 4" inches to allow for covering the corners.

Fold binding strips in half lengthwise with wrong sides together. Pin binding to quilt, having raw edges of quilt top and raw edges of binding even. Stitch through all thicknesses (binding, quilt top, batting and quilt back). Sew top and bottom bindings on first. Attach sides, sewing over top of extended bindings on upper and lower edges.

To sew binding on a scalloped edge, baste the raw edges of the quilt together. Mark the scallops. Sew the binding along the marked edge. Trim the scallops even with the edge of the binding. Wrap the binding around to the back, enclosing the raw edges and covering the stitch line. Slipstitch in place with thread that matches the color of the binding fabric.

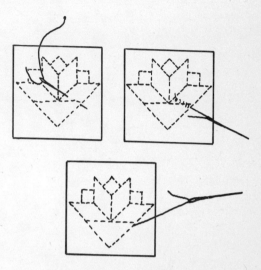

To both secure the quilting thread at the beginning and to hide the knot, insert the needle through only the quilt top, about one inch from where the quilting will begin, pull the thread through to the knot, and gently tug on the knot until it slips through the fabric and is lodged invisibly underneath the top.

To Display Quilts

Wall quilts can be hung in various ways. One is simply to tack the quilt directly to the wall. However, this is potentially damaging to both quilt and wall. Except for a permanent hanging, this is probably not the best way.

Another option is to hang the quilt like a painting. To do this, make a narrow sleeve from matching fabric and hand sew it to the upper edge of the quilt along the base. Insert a dowel rod through the sleeve and hang the rod by wire or nylon string.

The quilt can also be hung on a frame. This method requires velcro or fabric to be attached to the frame itself. In the case of velcro, one side is stapled to the frame. The opposite velcro is hand-sewn on the edges of the quilt and attached carefully to the velcro on the frame. If fabric is attached to the frame, the quilt is then handstitched to the frame itself.

Quilts can also be mounted inside plexiglass by a professional framery. This method, often reserved for antique quilts, can provide an acid-free, dirt-free and, with special plexiglass, a sun-proof environment for your quilt.

Signing and Dating Quilts

To preserve history for future generations, sign and date the quilts you make. Include your initials and the year the quilt was made. This data is usually added rather discreetly in a corner of the quilt. It can be embroidered, or quilted among the quilting designs. Another alternative is to stitch or write the information on a separate piece of fabric and handstitch it to the back of the quilt. Whatever method you choose, this is an important part of finishing a quilt.

The Country Bride Quilt

Cutting Lay-out for Queen-size or Double-size Quilt

Final size—approximately 92″ x 109″
Total yardage for quilt top—8⅞ yards
Total yardage for quilt back—6¼ yards plus 12″ left from cutting borders on front

Country Bride Applique Yardage Requirements

Hearts, bird wings and binding— 1¾ yards
Birds— ½ yard
Tulips— ½ yard
Tulip centers— ¼ yard
Leaves— ½ yards each of 2 fabrics
Tulip tips— ⅛ yard
Shades underneath heart— ¼ yard each of 5 shades

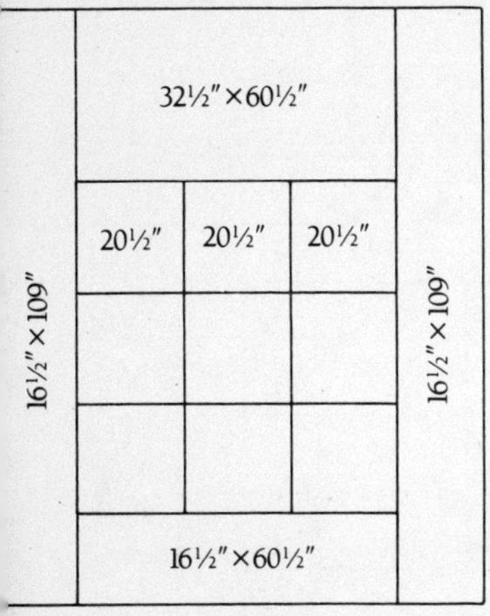

32½″×60½″
20½″
20½″
20½″
16½″×109″
16½″×109″
16½″×60½″

Side Borders
112″ × 45″ (3⅛ yards)

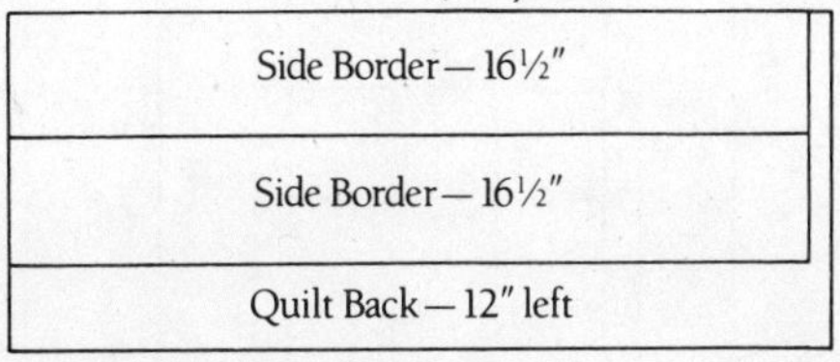

Side Border— 16½″
Side Border— 16½″
Quilt Back— 12″ left

Quilt Back (6¼ yards) plus 12″ left from cutting borders on front

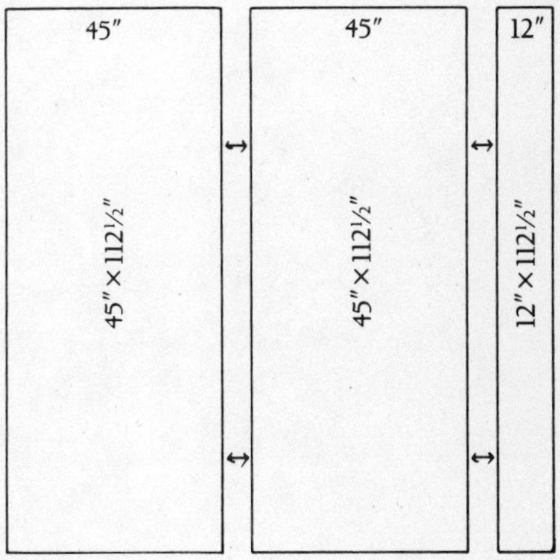

45″
45″
12″
45″×112½″
45″×112½″
12″×112½″

Patches, Bottom Border, Pillow throw (5¾ yards = 207″)

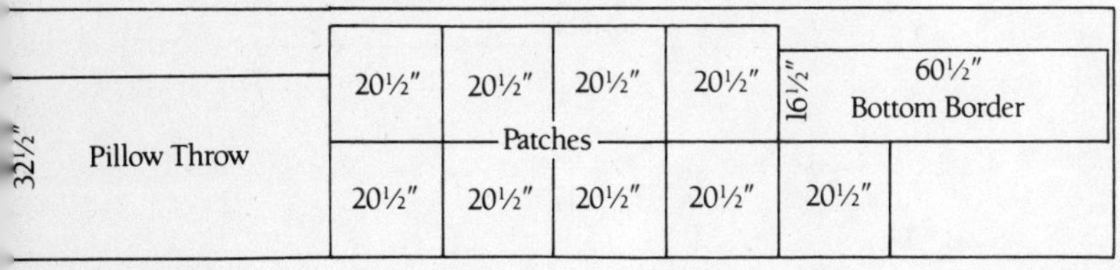

32½″
Pillow Throw
20½″
20½″
20½″
20½″
16½″
60½″
Bottom Border
Patches
20½″
20½″
20½″
20½″
20½″

Cutting Layout for King-Size Quilt

Finished size—approximately 110″ × 116″
Total yardage for quilt top—10¼ yards
Total yardage for back—10½ yards

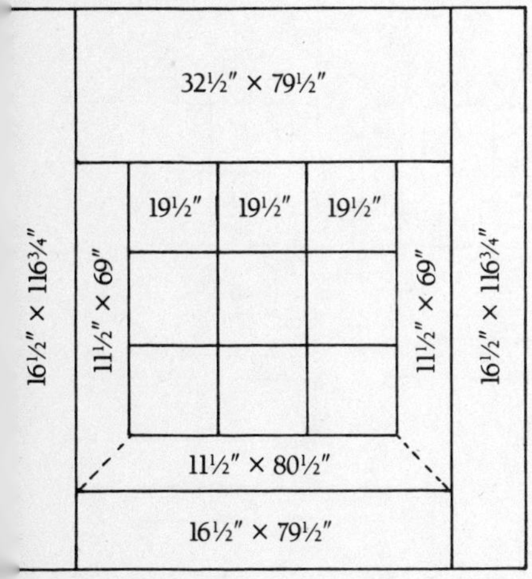

32½″ × 79½″
19½″
19½″
19½″
16½″ × 116¾″
11½″ × 69″
11½″ × 69″
16½″ × 116¾″
11½″ × 80½″
16½″ × 79½″

Lower Border and Patches (2¼ yards)

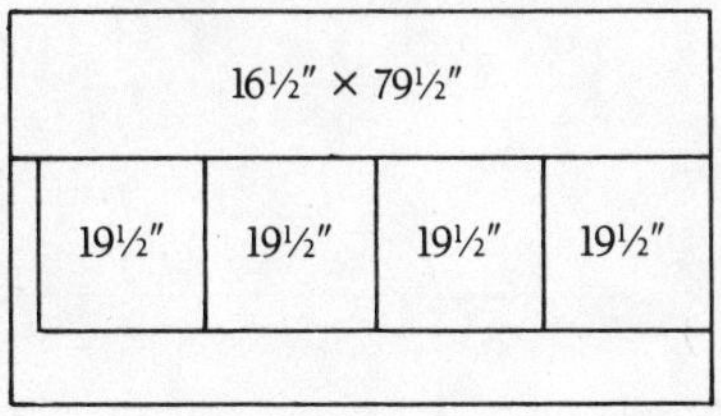

16½″ × 79½″
19½″
19½″
19½″
19½″

Quilt Back

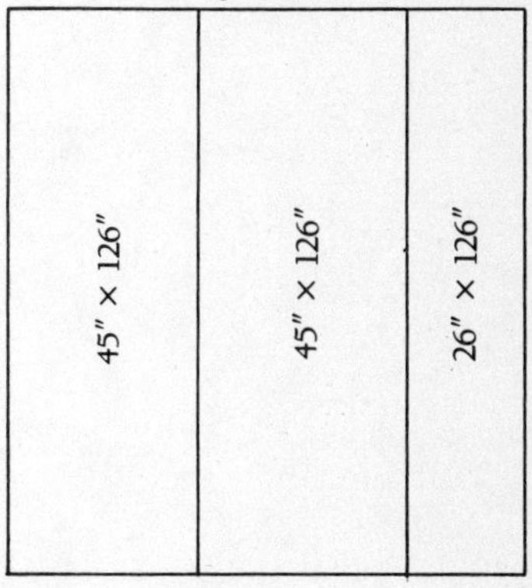

45″ × 126″
45″ × 126″
26″ × 126″

Borders and Inner Side Section (3½ yards)

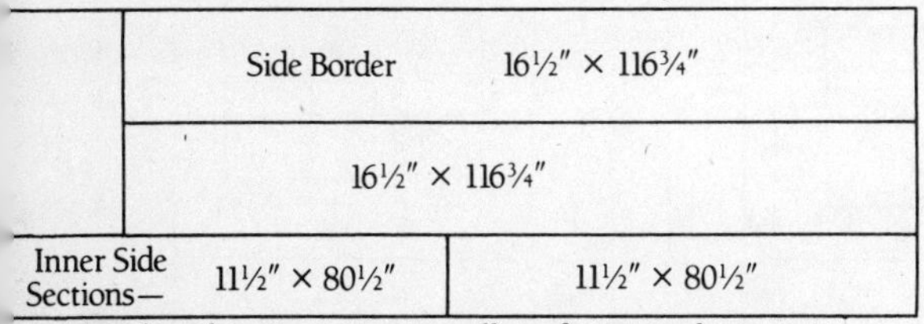

Side Border 16½″ × 116¾″
16½″ × 116¾″
Inner Side Sections—
11½″ × 80½″
11½″ × 80½″

(extra length on inner sections allows for mitered corners)

Pillow Throw and Lower Inside Section
(2¼ yards)

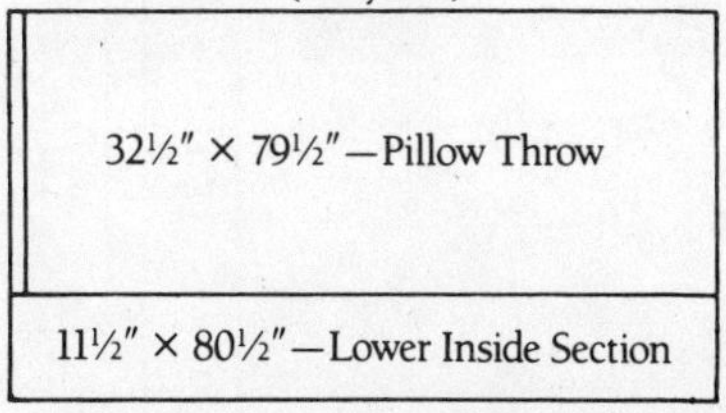

32½″ × 79½″—Pillow Throw
11½″ × 80½″—Lower Inside Section

Patches (1¾ yards)

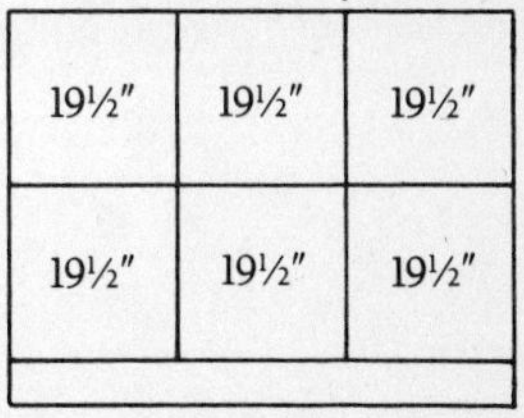

19½″
19½″
19½″
19½″
19½″
19½″

Queen size

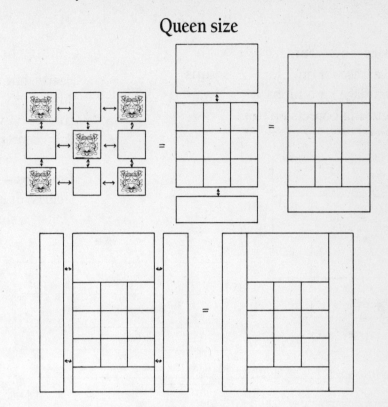

King size

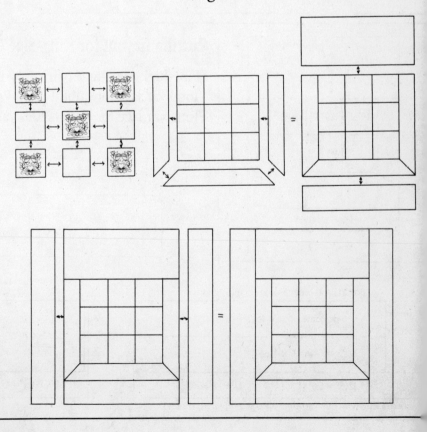

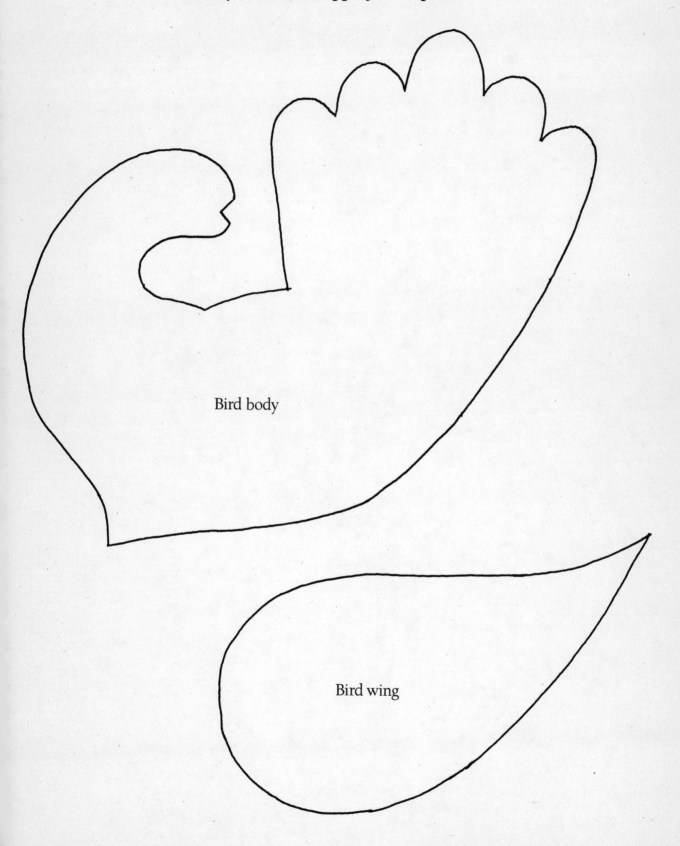

Bird body

Bird wing

Country Bride Quilt Applique Templates

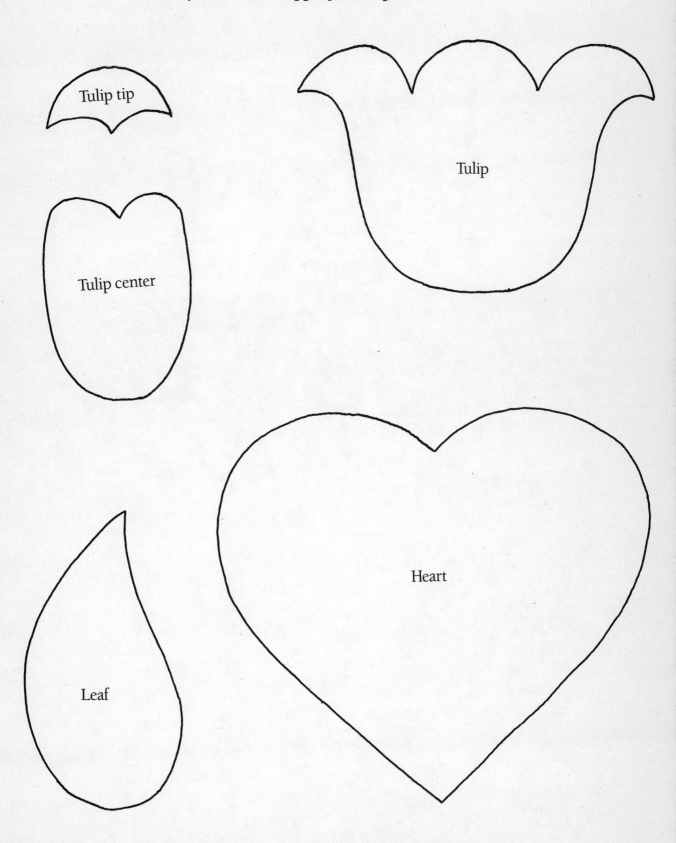

Tulip tip

Tulip

Tulip center

Heart

Leaf

Country Bride Quilt Applique Templates
Heart Fan Series

To create finished templates, match corresponding notches along dotted lines of Heart Fan Series and tape.
Completed template will look like this:

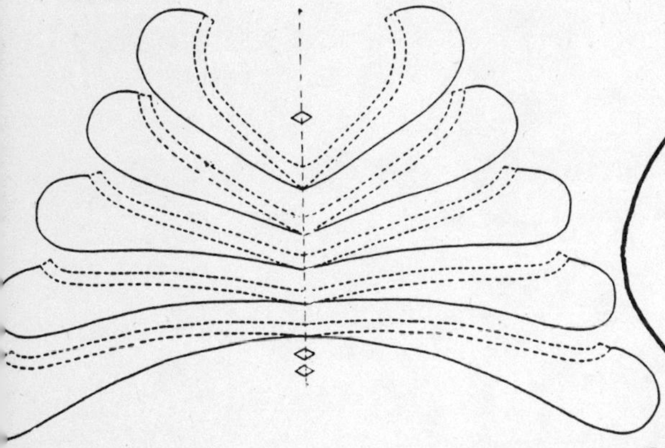

A

B

Cut along dotted line.

A

Cut along dotted line.

To create the finished outline, match corresponding letters and notches along dotted lines and tape. Completed Applique layout will look like this:

L

K

J

I

Trim along dotted line.

27

Country Bride Quilt Pillow Throw Applique Layout

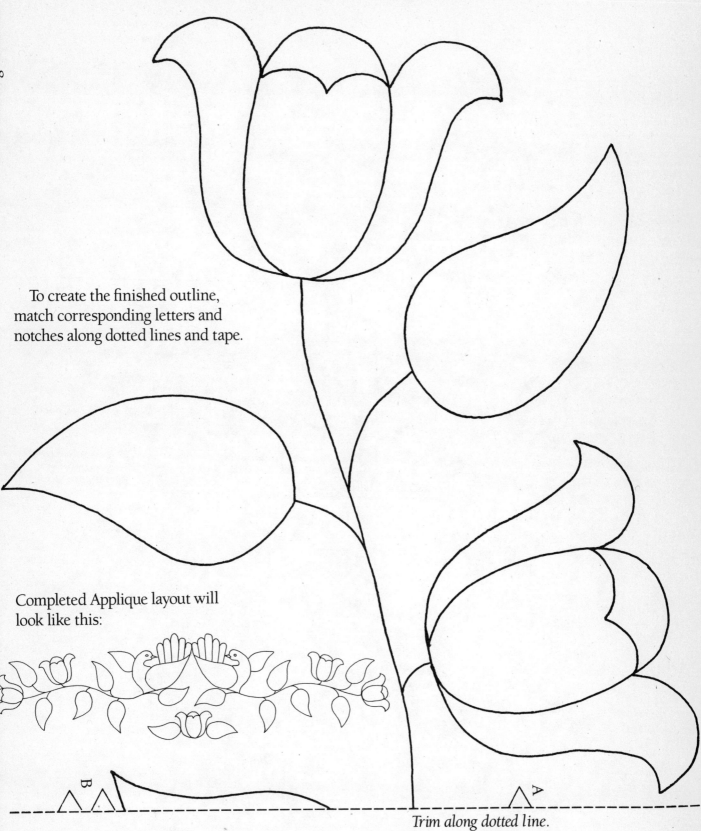

To create the finished outline, match corresponding letters and notches along dotted lines and tape.

Completed Applique layout will look like this:

B   A

Trim along dotted line.

43

Country Bride Quilt Pillow Throw Applique Layout

Trim along dotted line.

A

B

C

D

Trim along dotted line.

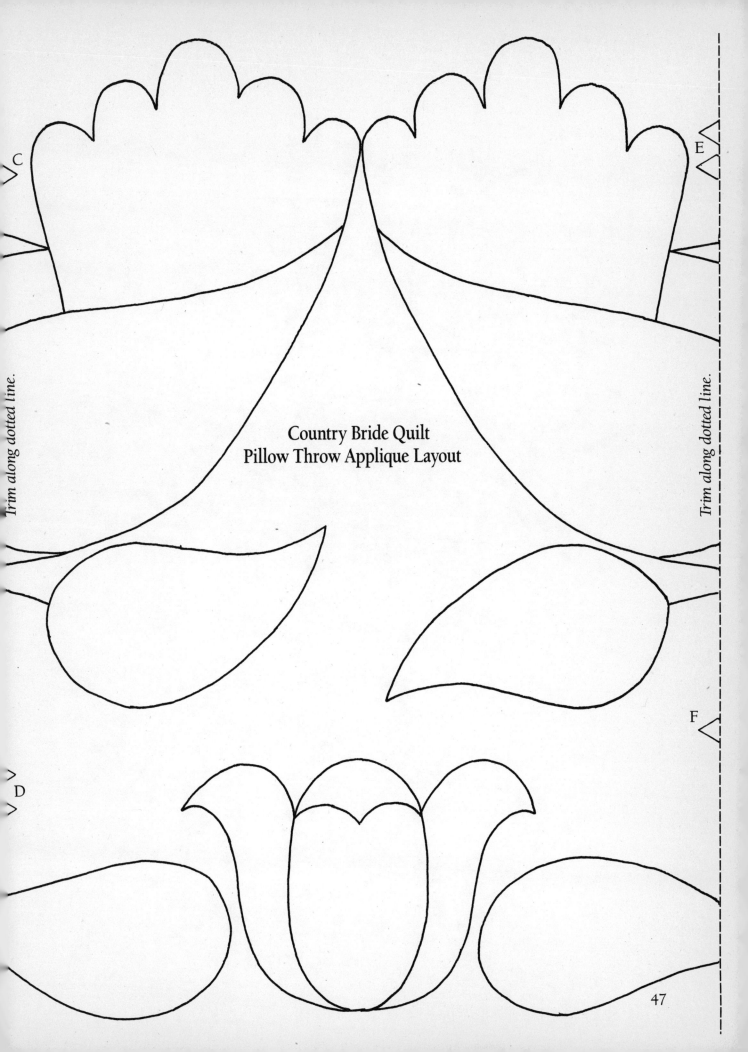

Country Bride Quilt
Pillow Throw Applique Layout

C

E

Trim along dotted line.

Trim along dotted line.

F

D

47

E

F

Trim along dotted line.

G

H

Trim along dotted line.

Trim along dotted line.

G

H

Country Bride Quilt Alternate Patch Quilting Template

To create the finished template, match corresponding letters and notches along dotted lines and tape.

Completed quilting template will look like this. Tulips are appliqued in corners.

53

Trim along dotted line.

B

C

A

Trim along dotted line.

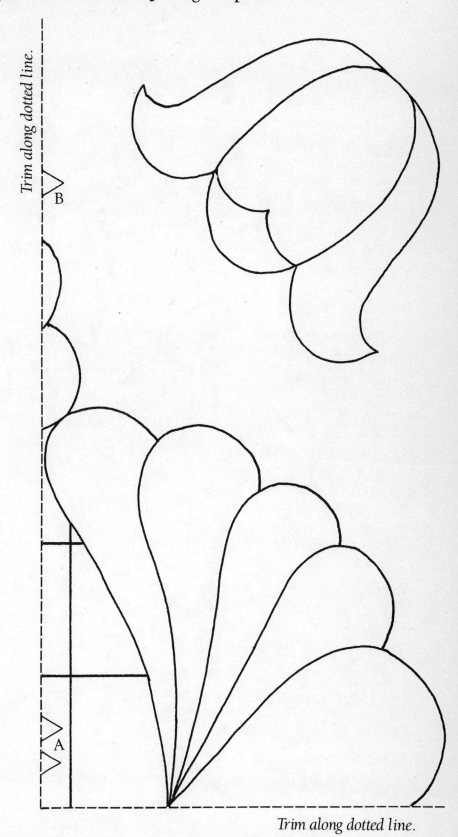

Trim along dotted line.

B

A

Trim along dotted line.

Country Bride Quilt Border Quilting Template

To create finished template,
match corresponding letters and
notches along dotted lines and tape.

A

Completed quilting template will
look like this:

B

59

A

**Country Bride Quilt
Border Quilting Template**

To create corner quilting, use as much of border quilting template as possible to achieve design shown on page 35.

B

Fabric requirements for Country Tulip Path Quilt

Tulip Centers, inner border, and binding — 2 yards
Sashing — 1 yard
Corner blocks (sashing and border) — 1½ yards
Tulip petals 1¼ yard print
        ¾ yard each of 2 solid colors
Leaves 1¼ yard
background and border 4 yards
backing 9 yards

Assembly instructions:

A – J — templates given

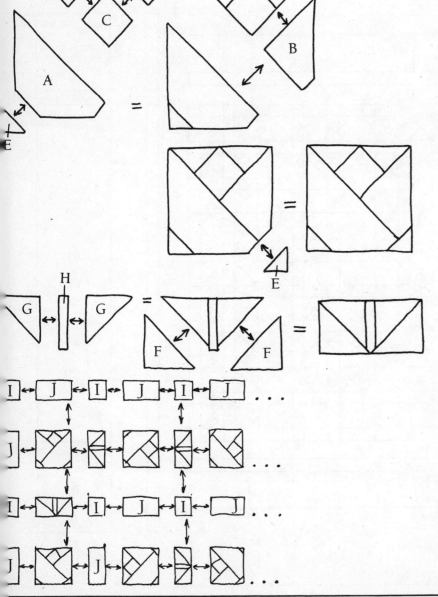

The Country Tulip Path Quilt

Approximate size 92 × 99

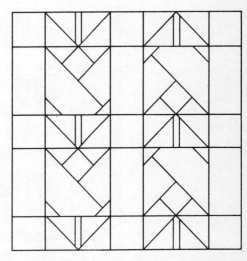

Assembly Instructions continued

Inner border—
    K—2¾" x 56¾"
    L—2¾" x 63½"
    M—2¾" x 16½"
Inner border corner blocks—
    O—2¾" x 2¾"
Outer border—
    P—16½" x 56¾"
    Q—16½" x 63½"
Outer border corner blocks—
    R—16½" x 16½"

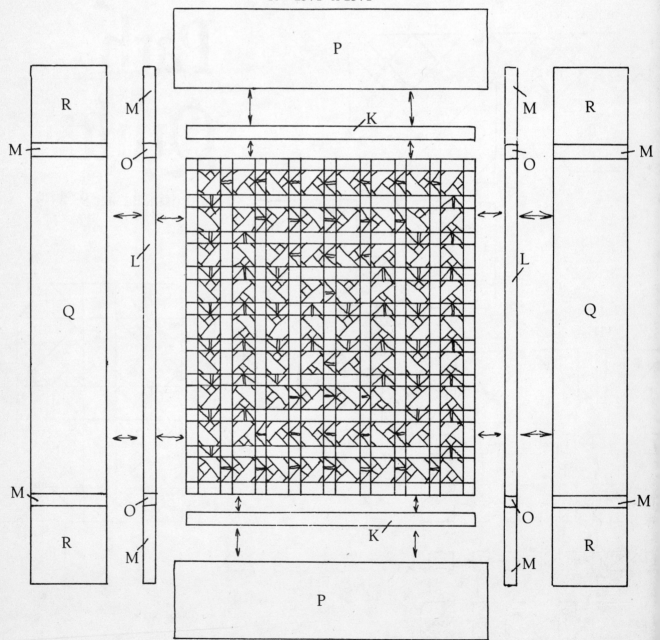

Country Tulip Path Piecing Templates

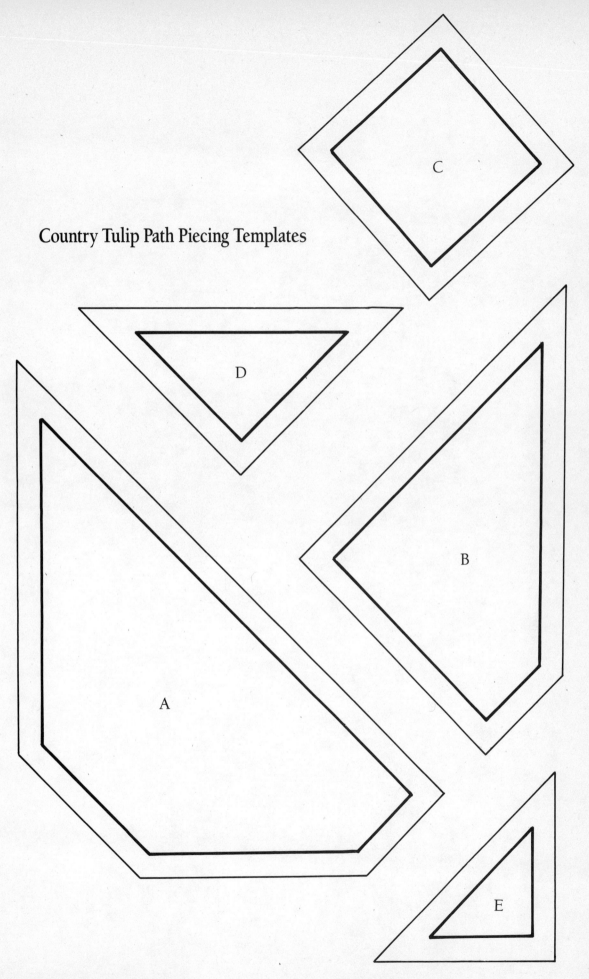

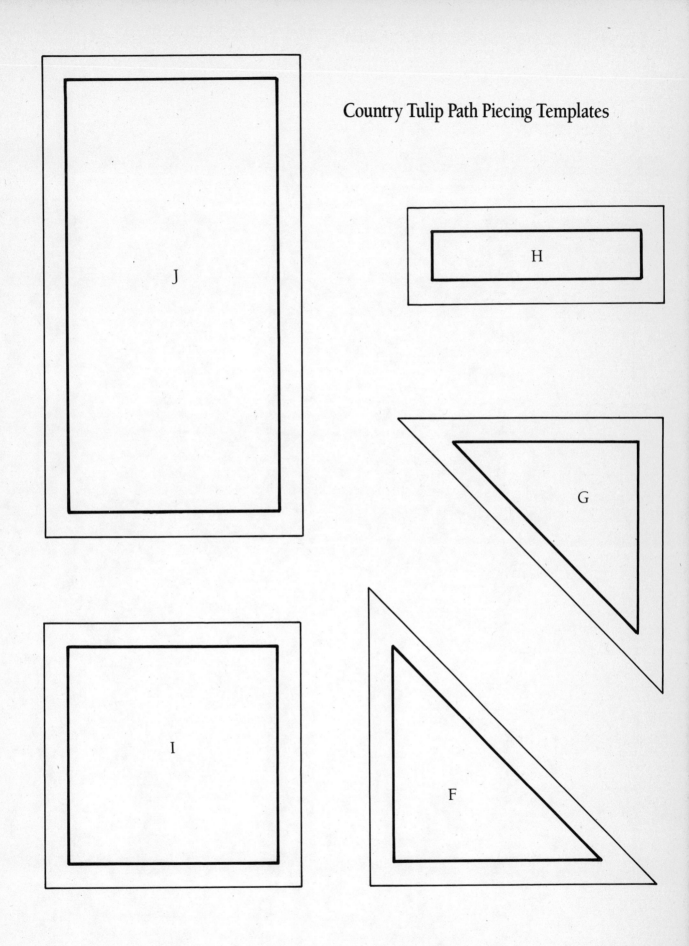

J

H

G

I

F

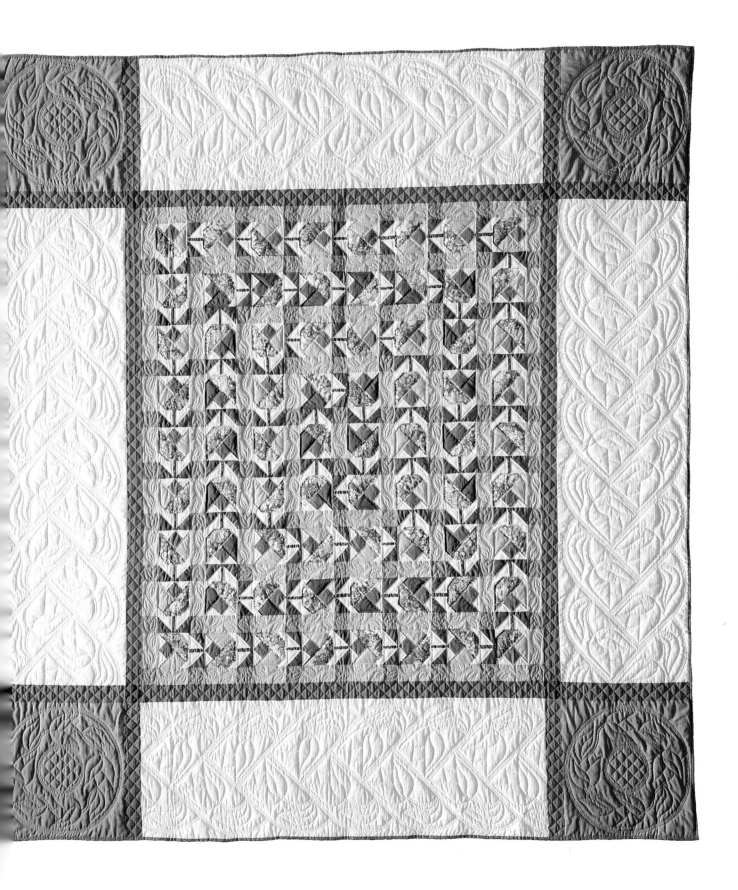

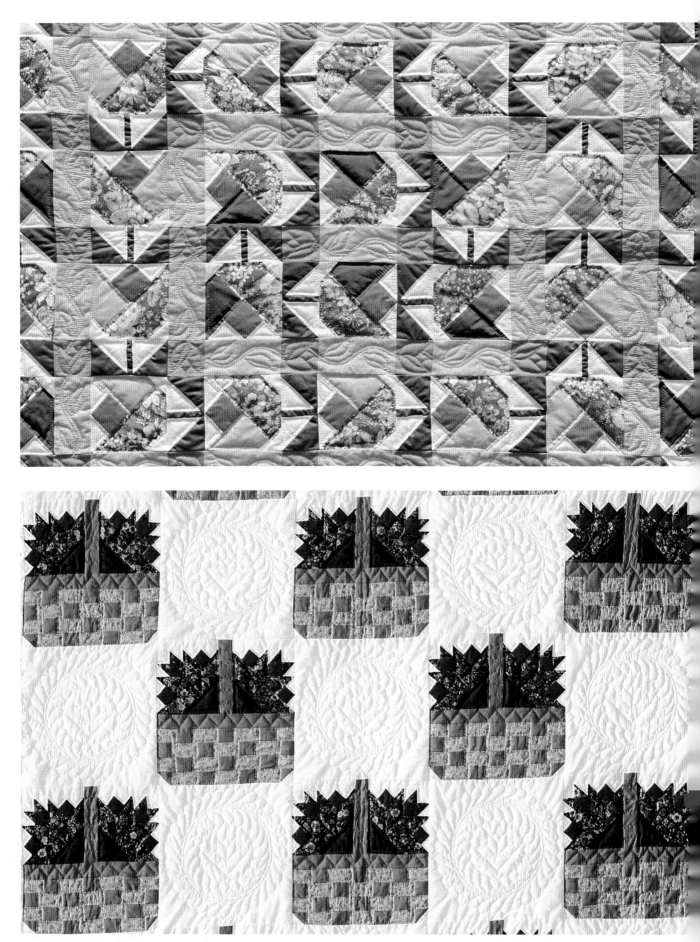

70

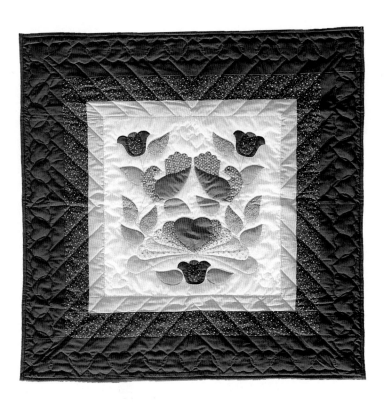

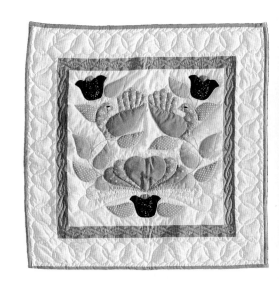

Country Tulip Path Sash Quilting Template

Trim along dotted line.

To create finished template, match corresponding letters and notches along dotted lines and tape.

Trim along dotted line.

A

B

A

B

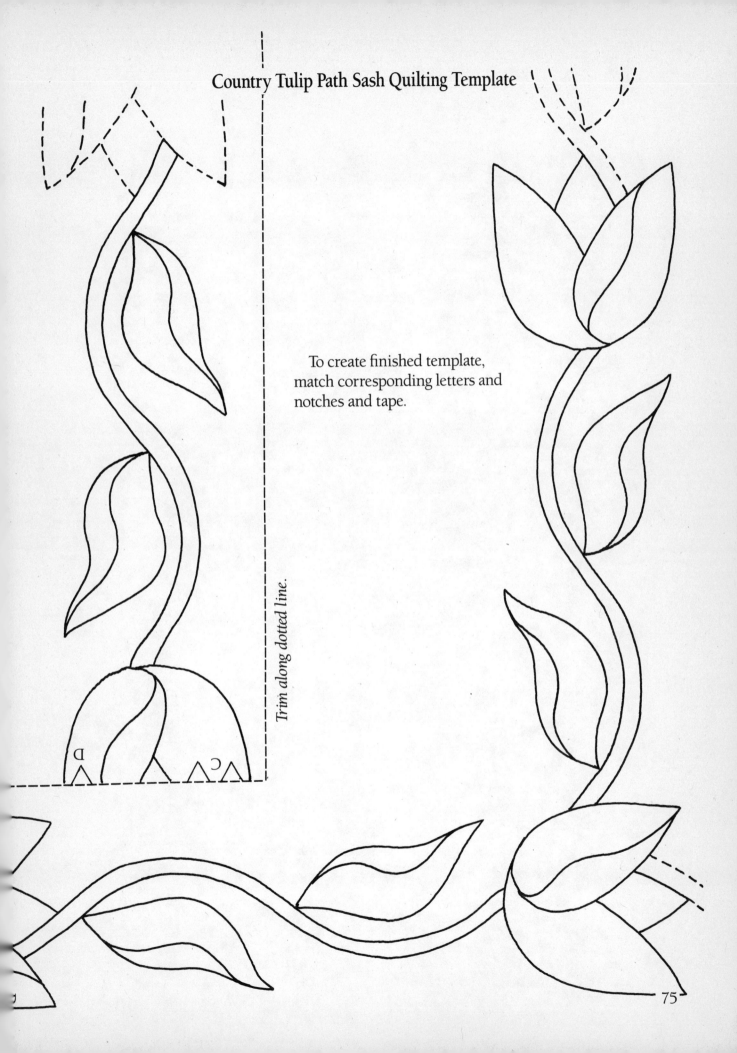

To create finished template, match corresponding letters and notches and tape.

Trim along dotted line.

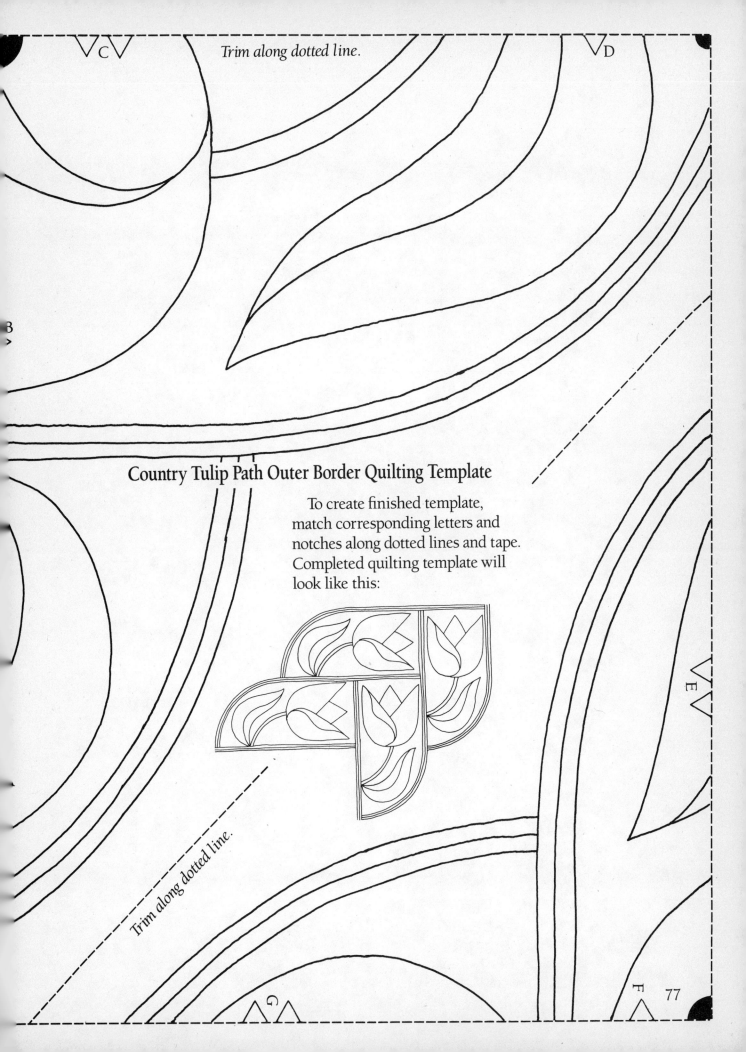

C D

B

Country Tulip Path Outer Border Quilting Template

To create finished template, match corresponding letters and notches along dotted lines and tape. Completed quilting template will look like this:

E

Trim along dotted line.

G

F

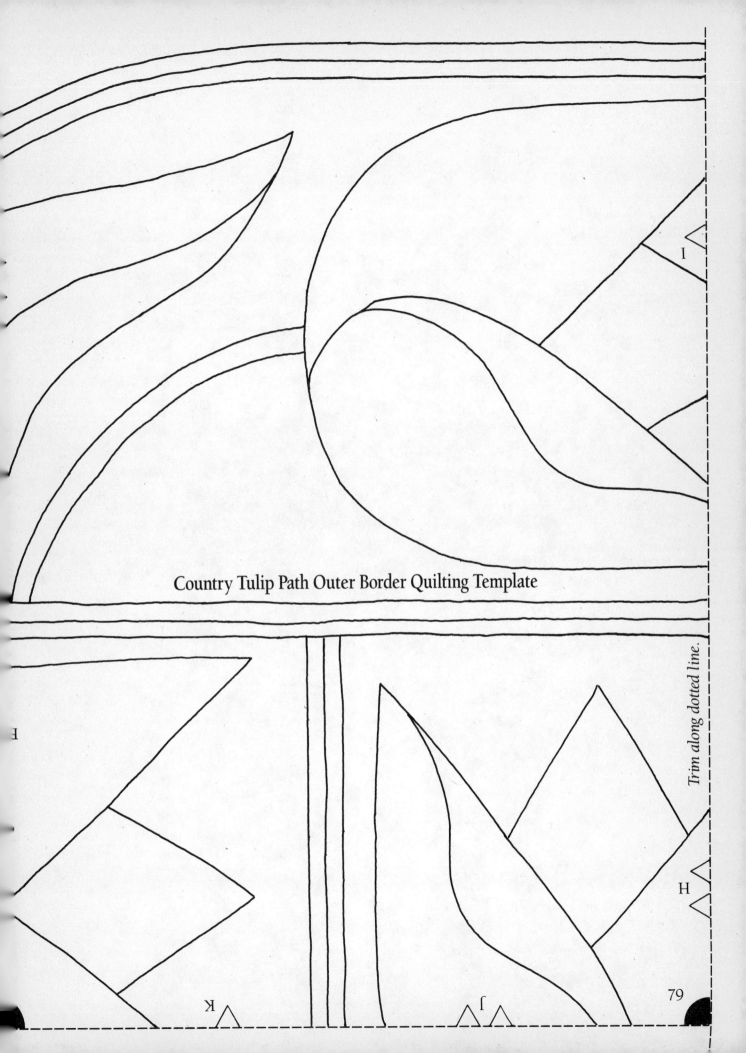

Country Tulip Path Outer Border Quilting Template

I

H

K   J

Trim along dotted line.

Country Tulip Path Outer Border Quilting Template

Trim along dotted line.

F

G

81

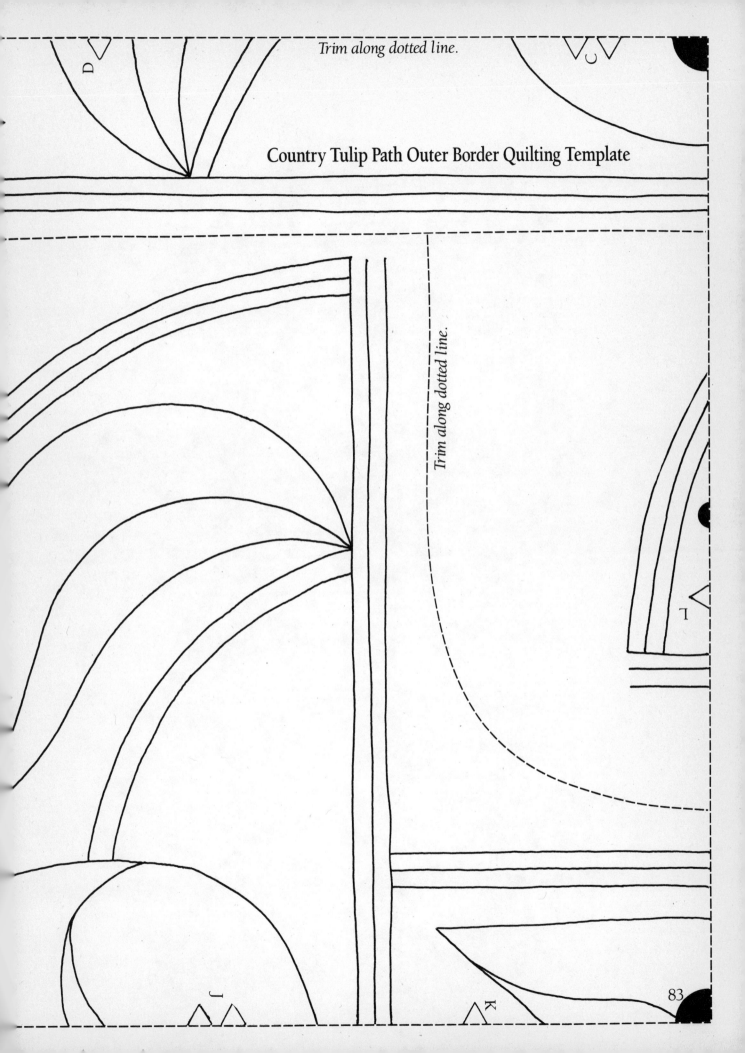

Trim along dotted line.

Country Tulip Path Outer Border Quilting Template

Trim along dotted line.

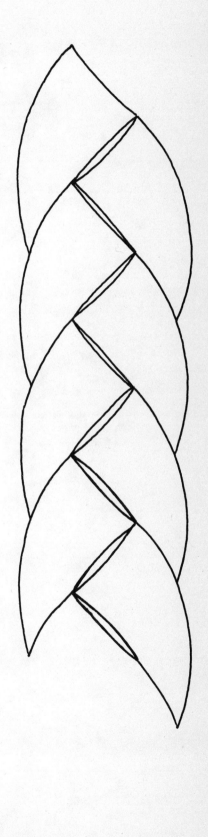

Trim along dotted line.

J

Country Tulip Path Corner Block Quilting Template

To create finished template, match corresponding letters and notches along dotted lines and tape. Completed quilting template will look like this:

Trim along dotted line.

Trim along dotted line.

I

Country Tulip Path Corner Block Quilting Template

Trim along dotted line.

C

D

B

A

89

Fabric Requirements for Country Flower Basket Quilt

Baskets and binding—1¾ yards solid fabric
   —¾ yard print fabric
Leaves and sawtooth border—¾ yard
Flower—1 yard print fabric
Flower tip and sawtooth border—¾ yard
Background—4 yards
Backing—9 yards

A–K templates given
L—template given (sawtooth)   N—2½″ x 56¾″
M—cut 27 squares 11¾″ x 11¾″   O—2½″ x 72″
P—use L template and sew together
   for sawtooth border to equal
   width and length of quilt top
Q—1½″ x 60¾″   R—1½″ x 76″
S—cut eight rectangles 5½″ x 11¾″
   and connect with alternating
   pieced and plain blocks
T—1½″ x 89¼″   U—1½″ x 102½″

The Country Basket Quilt

Approximate size—90″ x 102″

Assembly Instructions

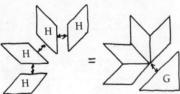

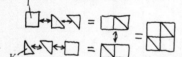

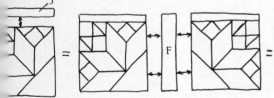
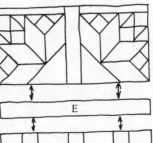

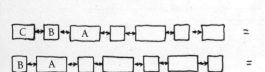
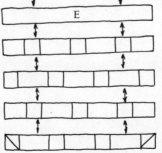

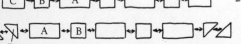

Drawing of completed patch

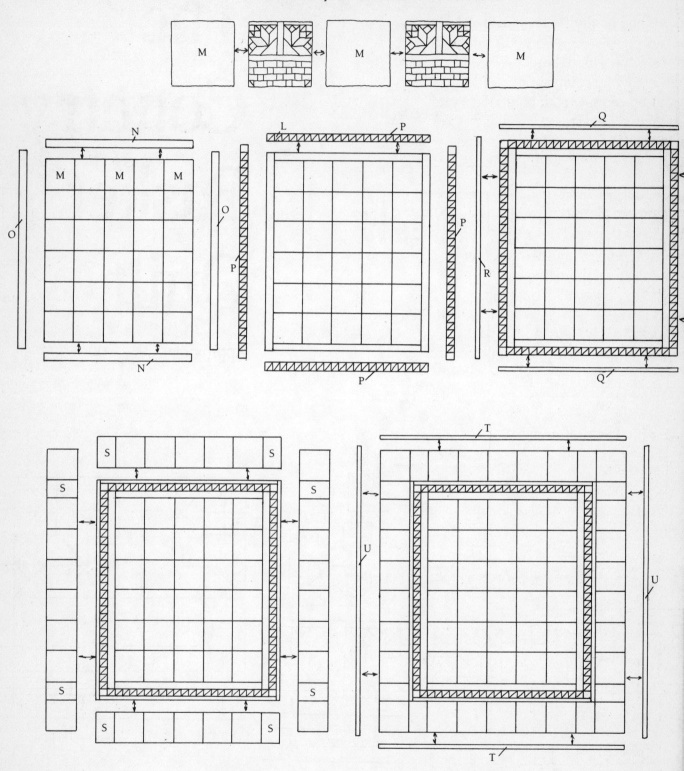

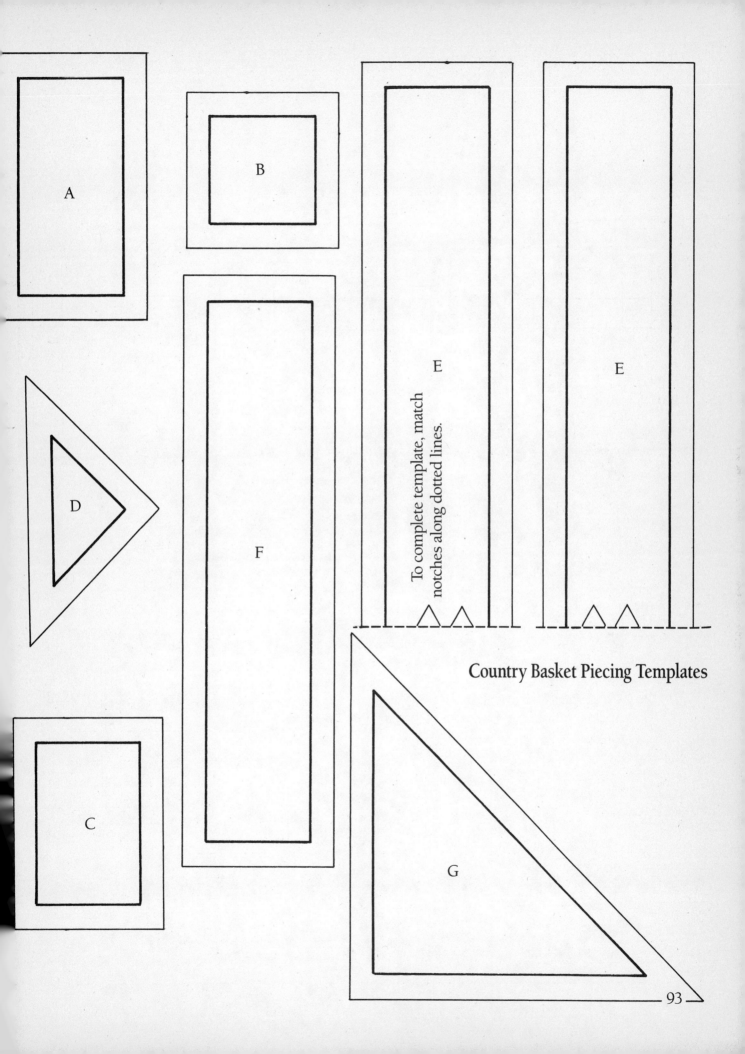

A

B

C

D

E

E

F

G

To complete template, match notches along dotted lines.

Country Basket Piecing Templates

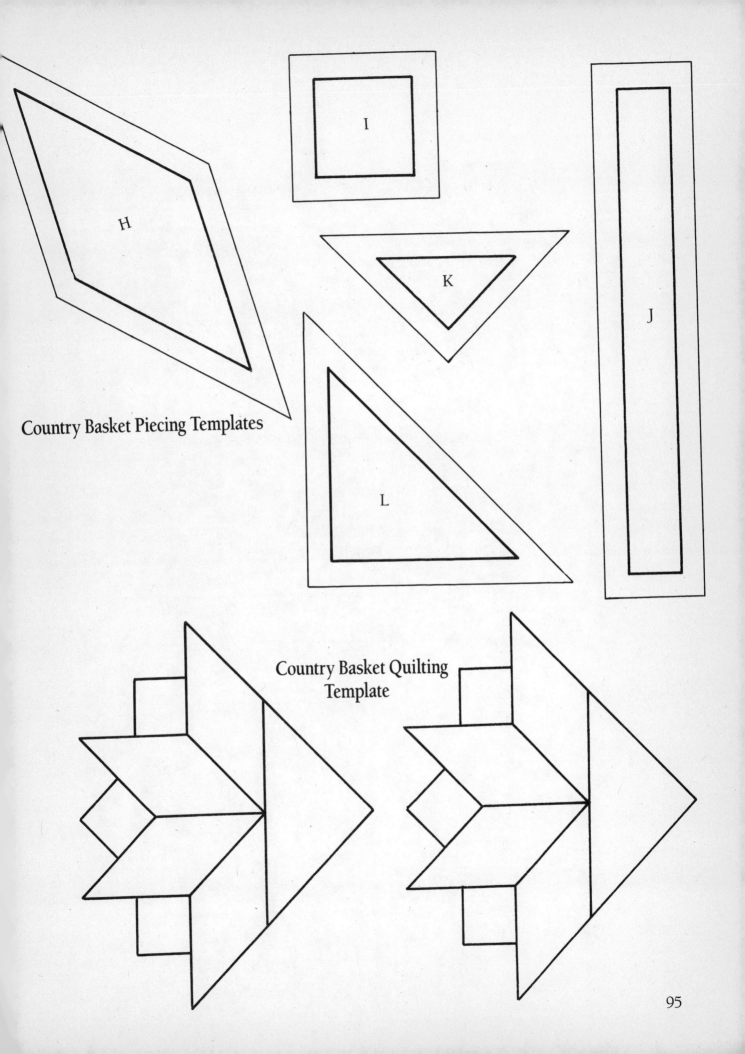

Country Basket Piecing Templates

H

I

K

J

L

Country Basket Quilting
Template

95

Country Basket Quilting Template

To complete template, match lines along dotted lines.

Completed template will look like this:

Trim along dotted line.

Trim along dotted line.

97

Country Basket Quilting Template

Trim along dotted line.

Trim along dotted line.

D

C

A

B

E

F

G

H

99

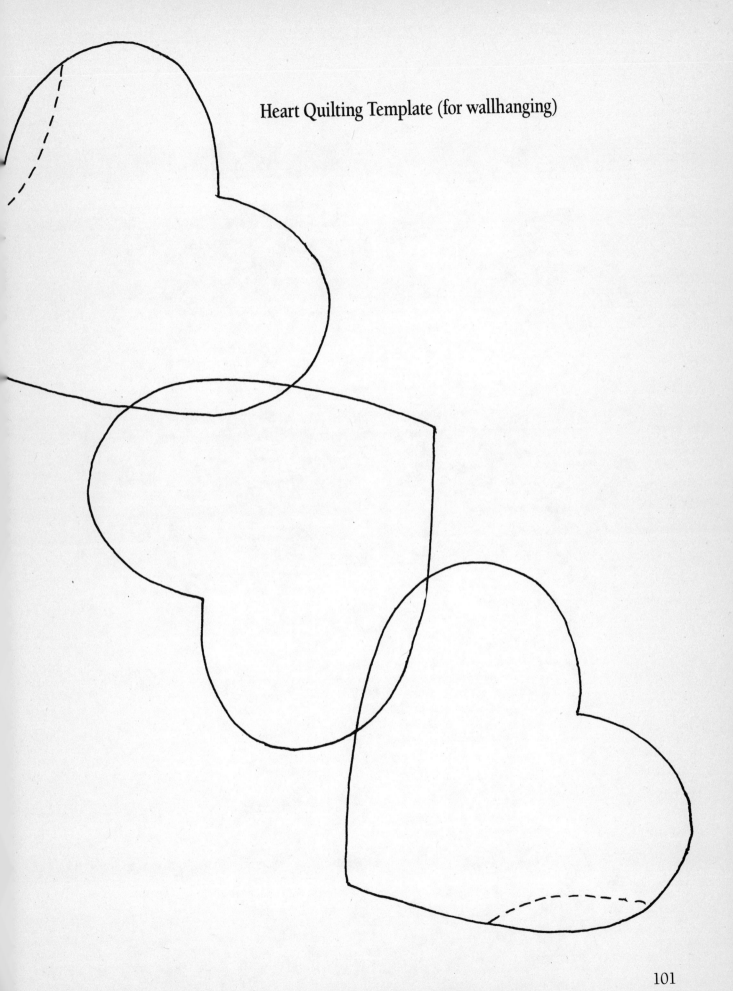

Heart Quilting Template (for wallhanging)

101

About The Old Country Store

Craig N. Heisey and Rachel T. Pellman are on the staff of The Old Country Store, located along Route 340 in Intercourse, Pa. The store offers crafts from more than 300 artisans, most of whom are local Amish and Mennonites. There are quilts of traditional and contemporary designs, patchwork pillows and pillow kits, afghans, stuffed animals, dolls, tablecloths and Christmas tree ornaments. Other handcrafted items include potholders, sunbonnets and wooden toys.

For the do-it-yourself quilter, the Store offers quilt supplies, fabric and a large selection of quilt books and patterns.

Located upstairs from the Store is The People's Place Quilt Museum. The Museum, which opened in 1988, features antique Amish quilts and crib quilts, as well as a small collection of dolls, doll quilts, socks and other decorative arts.

About the Authors

Craig N. Heisey and Rachel T. Pellman together developed The Country Bride Quilt, The Country Tulip Path Quilt and The Country Basket Quilt. They chose the fabric and supervised the creation of the original quilts, which were then made by Lancaster County Amish and Mennonite women.

Heisey lives in Mount Joy, Pa. He is art director for Good Enterprises, Intercourse, Pa.

Heisey and his wife, Linda, are the parents of two children.

Pellman lives in Lancaster, Pa., and is manager of The Old Country Store, Intercourse.

She is the author of *Amish Quilt Patterns* and *Small Amish Quilt Patterns,* co-author with Jan Steffy of *Patterns for Making Amish Dolls and Doll Clothes,* and co-author with her husband, Kenneth, of *The World of Amish Quilts, Amish Crib Quilts* and *Amish Doll Quilts, Dolls, and Other Playthings.*

The Pellmans are the parents of two sons.